THE GIFT OF
POSITIVITY

Cultivating10 Heartfelt Emotions to Create a Healthier, More Vibrant and Flourishing Life

Barbara E. Miller

First published in Australia in 2021 by:

Barbara E Miller
Potential Unlimited
PO Box 700
MAWSON ACT 2607
AUSTRALIA

http://www.potentialunlimited.com.au

This book is dedicated to Tony, Andy, and Nicole who light up my life with their eternal optimism and positivity.

Table of Contents

Introduction

In these challenging times, people are desperate to find new ways of adapting to change and uncertainty, coping with stress, anxiety, and depression. They want more control over their lives and are longing to be happier, healthier, and more fulfilled, especially after the coronavirus pandemic which has taken a huge toll on so many lives.

When things go wrong – you lose a loved one, get sick or face an uncertain future, resilience helps you persevere and bounce back stronger. It means surviving and thriving after difficult circumstances and using your strengths and inner resources to overcome the 'full catastrophe' and build a better life.

In *Full Catastrophe Living*, Jon-Kabat Zinn, says, "'Catastrophe' does not mean disaster. Rather it means the poignant enormity of our life experience." It includes crises and disasters like the pandemic, but also all the little things that go wrong and mount up. The good, the bad, and the ugly, and everything in between.

As a psychologist and transformational life coach, I am passionate about helping people – young and old, to use their strengths in new ways, to embrace the full catastrophe, and focus on what's right in life, rather than what's wrong. This is the new wave of positive psychology, which focuses on developing a growth mindset that accentuates the positive as well as the signature strengths needed to flourish.

When you are hit by adversity or have your life disrupted, how do you respond? Some people never get over stressful life events, so they languish. Unable to cope with the debilitating emotions that follow, they fall into pits of hopelessness and despair.

A few however, reach within themselves and find ways to cope by drawing on their inner strengths to survive and then thrive. When life gives them a lemon, they make lemonade, and flourish.

This book will help you to develop a growth mindset that accentuates the positive along with the key strengths to flourish.

What This Book Will Do for You

This book shows you how to create a *Positivity Portfolio* of 10 sometimes surprising forms of positivity that include joy, hope, amusement, serenity, and love. To benefit from this deeper layer of self-reflection you'll need to pull together objects and mementos that will create a heartfelt connection to the ten individual forms of positivity.

The idea of building these portfolios came to me after reading Barbara Frederickson's book on *Positivity,* which revealed surefire methods for creating a healthier, more vibrant, and flourishing life. When you accentuate the positive, you bounce back quicker from setbacks, connect with others, and become the best version of yourself. I have found this to be true in my own life and am keen to share those insights with you. However, to get the most out of this book you need to be ready for change and willing to coach yourself to create a better life.

To structure the creative process, I will guide you through the ten forms of positivity with real-life advice and coaching strategies for change. My suggestion is that you complete the weekly coaching tasks before moving forward. If you commit to daily mindfulness you will expand your own sources of positivity.

By the end of the challenge, you will have created a masterpiece to be proud of and, experience an 'upward spiral' of positivity to create a healthier, more vibrant, and flourishing life.

When you accentuate the positive, you bounce back quicker from setbacks, connect with others, and become the best version of yourself.

Flourishing to Build A Better Life

In *Positivity*, Barbara Frederickson, a distinguished Professor of Psychology, at the University of North Carolina, reveals the research behind a scientific formula which shows that when positive emotions outweigh negative emotions at a ratio of 3:1, people will flourish. This ratio has been proven to be a stable tipping point above which humans flourish and thrive. Anything below is an indicator of languishing, and a decline in human functioning and wellbeing.

The costs of languishing and losing vigor and vitality are high. For example, research showed that eighty percent of Americans score positivity ratios under 3 :1, which indicates they are languishing, and ratios of 1:0 are suggestive of depression. This is concerning as the increase in depressive ailments are now the leading cause of ill health and disability worldwide.[1]

However, thousands of peer-reviewed scientific papers prove that mindfulness, which is the practice of paying attention with deepened awareness, can improve mental and physical wellbeing while also enhancing creativity and the mental stamina required to build resilience and key strengths to flourish.[2]

In clinical terms, psychologists describe languishing as a, 'disorder experienced by negative people who describe their lives as hollow or empty.' Whilst they may not be clinically depressed, their lives lack meaning and purpose. Something is missing, and they want more.

Languishing means living a half-baked life that brings more emotional distress, excessive negative thinking, psychological problems, and dissatisfaction with life. Why would you want to live like that, when there is something you can do to accentuate the positive and flourish?

Flow — is a state of deep focus that occurs when you are totally engaged in challenging tasks that stretch your capacity to excel, such as creating a positivity portfolio. Flourishing on the other hand, is an ongoing thing which can happen when you identify and use your strengths to become the best version of yourself. At positivity ratios from 5:1 and up to 8:1, people are truly flourishing and following an upward trajectory in physical, emotional, cognitive, and social health. This is called resilience, which reflects a growth mindset that can adapt, change, and flourish.[3]

Resilience helps you persevere and adapt when things go awry. It gives you the ability to bounce back from difficult circumstances and includes qualities and protective factors to help build a better life and flourish.

When I was working as a transformational life coach and trainer, my positivity ratio used to be up around 7:1 most days, and I flourished by helping others seed positivity for transformational change.

You might enter flow with your hobbies. For example, golfing, surfing, gardening, writing, or playing a musical instrument. Successful leaders might experience flow while leading teams, improving a system, or creating a service for the greater good, by using strengths such as fairness, teamwork, and bravery.

"If you want to reshape your life for the better," writes Barbara, "the secret is not to grasp positivity too firmly, denying its transient nature. Rather, it's to seed more of it into your life – to increase your *quantity* of positivity over time."

By seeding positivity, you can transform your life from 'so-so to joyous,' through a process she calls 'the upward spiral,' which is heartfelt and more enduring than happiness. It turns out that positivity is the secret to becoming more resilient. Tracking and monitoring your positivity ratio over time is the key to flourishing for enduring fulfilment.

The Positivity Shift

The growth of positive psychology in the past decade has been astounding, and the mindfulness movement, phenomenal. In 1998, Martin Seligman at the University of Pennsylvania, predicted a change in psychology from a preoccupation with repairing the worst things in life, to building strengths to create a better one. The strengths include such qualities as: curiosity, gratitude, and hope — all aspects of flourishing.

However, negative thinking, and listening to your internal critic, (or monkey mind which rarely shuts up) prevents many of us from harnessing our true potential to flourish. Yet most of us are unaware of the damage a fixed mindset has on our wellbeing. Avoiding negative people, especially during tough times, and conserving your energy is important, as you need all the energy you can muster to flourish.

In the book *Mindset,* Carol Dweck, a leading expert in motivation and personality, discovered that it's our mindset that creates our mental world. She explains how and why we become optimistic or pessimistic, joyful, or depressed. A growth mindset shapes our goals, our attitudes, our relationships, how we raise our children, and is the best predictor of whether we will fulfil our potential, whereas depression is associated with a fixed-mindset, negative thinking and endless ruminations peppered with self-doubt, hopelessness, and fears that rob people of their drive to overcome adversity.

Everyone experiences flow from time to time; you might recognize its characteristics: you feel strong and alert, in effortless control, unselfconscious, and engaged fully in the activity. Emotional problems seem to fade away, and there is an exhilarating feeling of, "I can do this, yes, I can."

Love of learning is one of my top strengths, and I flourish whenever I'm mastering new skills, topics, or absorbing bodies of knowledge. For instance, I am currently completing an online Masters' Degree in Writing, and I'm feeling on top of the world. Getting published at 75 years of age was a challenge, but it filled my heart with absolute joy and pride, and my positivity ratio soared sky high. Flourishing is a fantastic feeling, better than a runner's high, and more enduring. Over the years I have gained attributes such as optimism, perspective, and creativity, by helping others overcome setbacks.

When you identify and use key strengths in challenging ways, you stretch your capabilities, boost neuroplasticity — the brain's ability to adapt and change — and become more engaged and fulfilled in life. The positive emotions, which are addictive, are more important than happiness which is fleeting.

In essence, flourishing is you at your best. The following coaching tools take you to a positivity psychology web site where you can assess your signature strengths and apply wisdom and positive mindsets.

A Taste of Mindfulness

Just in case you didn't known, mindfulness is the act of paying attention with moment-by-moment awareness, being non-judgmental, cultivating positive emotions, and accepting the good, the bad, and the ugly. It's not about looking at life through rose coloured glasses. Rather, it helps you to let go of the past and accept what you can and can't control with greater equanimity.

Many people use mindfulness to deal with chronic pain, destructive emotions, manage stress, anxiety, or depression. While others might use it to overcome a crisis or shine a light on their dark side for a spiritual transformation.

In recent years, scientists have discovered that practising mindfulness meditation for at least ten minutes a day can enhance creativity, problem solving and decision making, plus a host of other good things. With a little practice anyone can do it and the profound benefits lead to an increased sense of happiness and wellbeing: increased clarity of mind, increased productivity, and better health.

More recent studies reveal different meditation pathways that can be placed on a spectrum from 'deep to wide' practices that range from Theravada Buddhism as practised by Tibetan monks such as the Dalai Lama, to mindfulness-based stress reduction programs (known as MBSR) or Mindfulness Based Cognitive Therapy (MBCT) with practices removed from the spiritual context and adapted for the West.[4]

At the far end of the spectrum are the even more widely accessible forms of meditation, the most watered-down versions, for sleep, anxiety, or stress, which renders them readily available and appealing to many.

Despite the value of meditation as a tool for enhancing wellbeing, people with serious mental health issues are advised to consult their doctor or psychiatrist before embarking on a mindfulness meditation program. However, from my perspective as a psychologist and practitioner with over twenty years of meditation experience, the relaxation and wellbeing benefits have been life changing.

If you wish to begin a mindfulness program to improve your mental and physical wellbeing, and at the same time enhance your creativity, mental stamina, and resilience whilst creating your Positivity Portfolio, I recommend the following online meditation programs.

CHALLENGE TO DO NOW

Mindfulness Meditation

Whilst there is no one-program-fits-all, I recommended one of the following:

- The Healthy Minds Free App - to boost wellbeing and life satisfaction: https://apps.apple.com/us/app/healthy-minds-program
- The Insight Timer Free App - for sleep, anxiety, stress, and ambient music: https://insighttimer.com

You will need a smart phone to download the app and earphones to tune into the meditation program or playlist. Insight Timer also features an eclectic mix of ambient music that will enhance your creative process and wellbeing.

Select your program, meditate for at least 10 minutes a day, and track your positivity ratio over time.

Creating a Positivity Portfolio

It's time now to begin creating your unique portfolio and gather resources that include images of people, places, or things designed to showcase each of the ten positive emotions which are:

1. Joy – creating pleasure and playfulness to shine
2. Gratitude – giving thanks and expressing appreciation
3. Serenity – finding peace and contentment in a frantic world
4. Interest – arousing curiosity and willingness to grow
5. Hope – cultivating optimism and intention to flow
6. Pride – boosting confidence and self-satisfaction to excel
7. Amusement – savoring fun and laughter to enjoy life
8. Inspiration – seeking elevation and exuberance to change
9. Awe – being transfixed by wonder and beauty
10. Love – experiencing warmth, connection, and the greatest gift of all.

While other forms surely exist, research suggests that these ten forms of positivity influence people's day-to-day lives the most.[5] When you focus on these forms of positivity, you put the brakes on negativity and reach a tipping point or a 'sweet spot' in between where a small change, like expressing gratitude for instance, makes a big difference. This is the gift of positivity.

Throughout the creative challenge, you will draw on memories and activities that combine to broaden and build your resilience, using mindfulness and key strengths to overcome adversity, and flourish in your little corner of the world.

The purpose of creating a 'Positivity Portfolio' is to have a sense of the people, places and things that light you up, thus drawing upon the power of creation to flourish more and languish less. To structure the process, I will guide you through each of the ten positive emotions with examples and coaching questions to help you create a masterful portfolio that will accentuate the positivity in your life.

Throughout the process I want you to get to know each emotion personally, to dig deep and discover how it plays out in your life. The beauty of emotions is that they are highly personal and apt to change. What makes one person serene, may be totally lost on another. Likewise, what amuses one friend might upset another. This means that each person's pathway to flourishing will be unique.

Decide which emotion you wish to seed and focus on and elicit the positive emotions aroused during the day. The imagery you create, which works on a sub-conscious level, will prompt the necessary action you need to take to boost your positivity ratio overtime. It is suggested that you work on each emotion for a week to embed the effects. Then put your insights into practice.

For instance, joy might prompt you to plan dinners with friends, and use your social intelligence and humor to host a dinner party. The following week you might choose serenity and go on a retreat to practice mindfulness. Or plan a weekend getaway to use key attributes such as gratitude, kindness, or spirituality to create a better life.

Ongoing research shows very clearly that we can reduce our 'negativity bias,' — the phenomenon by which we give more psychological weight to bad experiences than good ones — by broadening and building positive emotions that give us more pleasure and less pain.

Format and Design

Your portfolio can take any of these forms:

- A large Artists Visual Diary or black display portfolio with plastic sleeves
- Scrapbook or cardboard sheets that can be laminated for your wall

- Photographic albums, vision boards or mind maps with symbols
- A beautifully bound journal for self-reflection and action plans for change
- Gift boxes, baskets, or box files to fill with treasured objects and memories.

Whatever you decide, it needs to be easily accessible, portable, and enjoyable. Imagine you are an 'artist in residence' and each emotion is a work of art in progress. The visual images you create – photos, memorabilia, pictures, poems etc., and the emotions aroused, will inspire you to cultivate more positivity by focusing on what you desire to build a more fulfilling and flourishing life.

As the goal of positive psychology is to increase flourishing as opposed to languishing, its core teachings center around the **PERMA** model which represent five core elements:

- **P**ositive Emotions
- **E**ngagement
- **R**elationships
- **M**eaning and
- **A**ccomplishments. [6]

As you develop your unique portfolio, you will tap into these elements by applying the coaching challenges and mindfulness practices to create a healthier, more vibrant, and flourishing life.

Remember you are tapping into a positivity well, so lighten up, have fun, and enjoy the process.

The purpose of creating a 'Positivity Portfolio' is to have a sense of the people, places and things that light you up and draw upon the power of creation to flourish more and languish less.

CHALLENGE TO DO NOW

Tips to Spark Creativity

People often tell me they are not creative. Or they are unable to visualize their goals. If you are one of those people, you might like to choose any of the following as a practical way of cultivating positivity over time.

- Create a playlist on Spotify and listen to a series of 10 *Positive-Optimistic Songs* at set times each week
- Plan a 10-Day Menu and serve up delectable dishes with edible gold leaf for joy or cake decorations, and share the positive vibes with family and friends
- Try your hand at sculpting images with clay, decorate a room with themed objects, or plant an herb garden named after each emotion
- Design a patchwork quilt, embroider a collection of baby clothes for loved ones or make character dolls that represent each emotion
- Plant sunflower seeds or exotic flowers in the Autumn and envision the positive emotions arising when your garden blossoms in the Spring.

Setting the Scene and Reflection

Before beginning, you might like to set up a quiet space and gather a selection of creative resources. These could be art materials, old magazines, family photos, etc. Create an ambient atmosphere, declutter, and play inspiring music to spark creative ideas.

Record your insight in a *Reflective Journal* and use it to track your positivity ratio, record insights and articulate your goals. During reflection you might like to jot down an incident or problem troubling you; break it into smaller parts and ask why each one is important. Draw on your positive insights and decide how you might set and achieve affirmative goals for transformational change.

Remember you are tapping into a positivity well, so lighten up, have fun, and enjoy the process.

A Personal Portfolio

The following is an example of a 'portfolio page' I created in a Visual Art Diary, which still brings an afterglow of joy and happy memories shared with family and friends. The images were assembled on an A5 page and decorated with paints and ink pens.

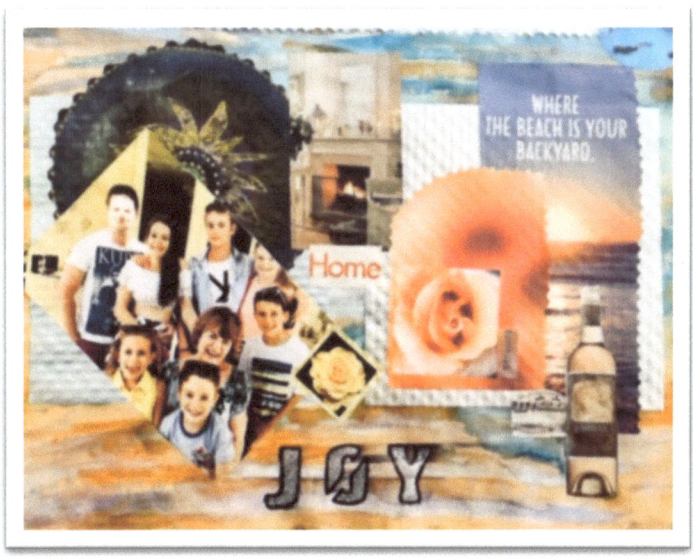

Figure 1: Positivity Portfolio collage depicting what joy means for me.

More recently, I created another portfolio based on the PERMA model of wellbeing with art therapist Janet McLeod, as a way of cultivating positivity and building resilience during the dark days of the coronavirus pandemic in 2020, when the death rate was escalating out of control, and the 'negativity bias', was thick in the air.

During this time, the bad news was overwhelming, and people lived in a constant state of fear and anxiety. However, each week I joined in with the group activities online and created images that boosted my positivity and led to an outpouring of creativity that left me singing in the shower and engaged with life.

To build resilience, I increased my daily dose of mindfulness, went for long walks on the beach, watched more sunsets, listened to the birds singing, and used strengths to follow my bliss the mindful way, creating art and writing a memoir.

Over time my positivity ratio increased from 3 to 5:1, which indicated I was flourishing despite the doom and gloom in the world. I have since created a series of the 'mindful art' projects to flourish the mindful way into the third age.

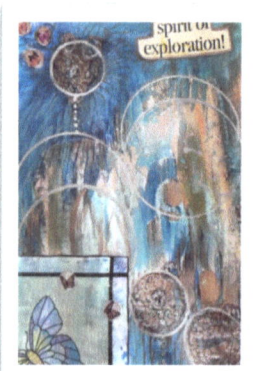 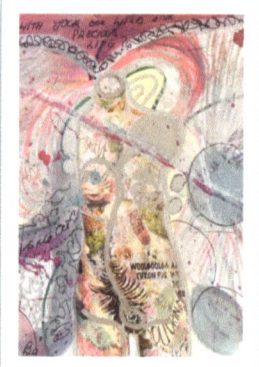 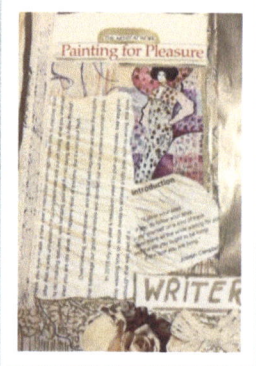

Figure 2: Positivity Portfolio images created during the coronavirus pandemic.

As Henry Ford once said, "If you think you can do a thing, or think you can't, you're right." What is your highest aspiration? And what do you need to do to build a better life?

There is no right or wrong way for you to create your positivity portfolio. Do whatever feels right for you and trust the process. Whether you choose to depict your 10 positive emotions in writing, painting, poetry, music, dance, or life, you can rest assured that 'there is a higher intelligence guiding your will to create and flourish the mindful way.' [7]

Ready? Then let's begin the process of creating your positivity portfolio.

There is no right or wrong way for you to create your positivity portfolio. Do whatever feels right for you and trust the process.

Week 1: JOY

Joy is not in things it is in us.

Richard Wagner

'Happiness lies in the joy of achievement and the thrill of creative effort,' writes Franklin D. Roosevelt. Yet happiness and joy mean different things to different people. To one person, it might mean making a lot of money, becoming a CEO, or having a thriving business. To another it might mean having loving relationships with family and friends, or the joy of having a longed-for child or grandchild.

Joy is a vivid emotion of pleasure and playfulness. It is an intense emotion that makes you feel joyful, blissful, or extremely happy. A source of joy can come from something that gives you pleasure or satisfaction: being engaged to be married, walking the Camino, a surprise birthday party, or getting a book published.

When I ask clients what brings them joy, it is something they need to think about. Joy like happiness, means different things to different people. For example:

- Doing all I can each day to make our house a home. Productive work and a balanced life with less chaos fills me with joy
- Listening to music, walking the dog first thing in the morning, or eating Swiss chocolate is a joyful experience
- Climbing a mountain, dinner with friends or playing with my kids brings an inner glow that lingers. Is that joy?

Joy feels light and bright. There is a spring in your step and your eyes sparkle. You feel like taking it all in, savoring the moment and reliving the memory over and over in your mind's eye. Above all joy fills you with delight, pleasure, or bliss. It is one of the most cherished emotions you can experience in life. Mark

Twain said, 'To get the value of joy you must have someone to divide it with.'

My children bring me absolute joy. My grandchildren make me jump for joy. Telling stories that capture their imagination taps into my sense of playfulness and creates an unstoppable smile. Having dinner with friends, a surprise birthday party or family event makes me feel light-hearted and in the moment. Joy fills me with delight.

How about you? Who and what brings you joy?

For your 'joy' portfolio, close your eyes for a few moments, and recall:

➢ People, places, and events where you felt happy, joyful and in the moment
➢ Happy memories you treasure. Who were you with and what were you doing?
➢ Times when you felt truly relaxed and light-hearted with a spring in your step
➢ Situations when you felt childlike with an unstoppable smile on your face
➢ Occasions when you experienced absolute joy, pleasure, or ecstasy.

Gather images, photos and expressions of joy and consider what you need to do more often to savor JOY. Listen to Beethoven's *Ode to Joy* and decide which strength you need to muster to bring more joy into your life. Is it curiosity, kindness, or love? Keep this in mind as you create your joy portfolio.

At the end of the week measure your positivity ratio and gauge your progress. If no change, reflect and ask yourself what do I need to do to feel more joyful?

CHALLENGE TO DO NOW

Three Good Things

Studies in positive psychology have shown that by identifying and using your strengths in new ways, expressing gratitude, and focusing on the good things that happen each day, you can reduce depression and boost happiness.

1. Select one of your top strengths and use it in a new way. For instance, if it's love you could plan a family reunion to show you care and get closer to others
2. Keep a gratitude diary and write down three things you are grateful for. It could be as simple as hot buttered toast. Or grand like acknowledging lifesavers
3. For the next 21 days, record three good things that happened the day before and savor the positivity. For instance, a message from a friend could trigger feelings of love and acceptance.

Books: *Stumbling on Happiness* by Daniel Gilbert, *The Book of Joy* by The Dalai Lama and Desmond Tutu or *Big Magic* by Elizabeth Gilbert

Movies: *Field of Dreams*, *Midnight in Paris*, *Samsara* or *The Wizard of Oz*.

Week 2: GRATITUDE

Wear gratitude like a cloak, and it will feed every corner of your life.

Rumi

Thank you. Two words that can make the world of difference for both the giver and receiver. Gratitude is a feeling of thankfulness or appreciation. When you give or receive a gift, or share rewarding experiences, you feel happy and grateful.

When someone does something nice or unexpected for you, it feels wonderful. It could be a phone call or a visit when you are sick or feeling down, or a stranger pays your parking meter when you do not have change. These simple acts of kindness tend to generate warm feelings of appreciation.

Gratitude is a key strength that leads to happiness. When you have it, you are aware of good things happening, and you never take them for granted. Marcel Proust said, "Let us be grateful to people who make us happy; they are the charming gardeners who make our souls blossom."

Whilst you might feel overwhelmed with gratitude at times, feeling and expressing gratitude are two different things. After coaching, Sarah expressed her gratitude in a card: *'I want to say thank you and tell you how much I have enjoyed this journey … you have made a real difference in my life.' My positivity ratio soared.*

Written expressions of gratitude contribute to my sense of belonging and making a difference. How about you? When was the last time you expressed gratitude or said, "Thank you"? When you express gratitude your positivity ratio soars.

For my son's 40th birthday, I gave him a gratitude letter expressing appreciation for his support during challenging times. He passed on the letter idea to his son who passed it on at college. During a boy's camp, students exchanged letters of gratitude to each other expressing their qualities and attributes, which left many basking in the afterglow of gratitude and appreciation. Sharing prolongs the gratitude experience which broadens and builds resilience.

However, gratitude has an evil twin — indebtedness which can make you feel you have to pay back acts of kindness begrudgingly to keep face. Or return a favor which feels unpleasant. Gratitude is more about giving freely and spontaneously without expectation.

When was the last time you expressed gratitude, felt thankful or showed heart felt appreciation? How might you use gratitude more often to flourish?

For your 'gratitude' portfolio:

➢ Think about occasions when you felt grateful or thankful, deeply appreciative of someone who did something significant or made an impact on your life
➢ What gifts do you treasure most? What inspires you to get creative about giving back?
➢ Bring to your mind a time when you received positive feedback for a job well done. Copy or recall the words spoken and add them to your portfolio.

Write down 10 good things you are grateful for. Add images of these good things to your portfolio and note how gratitude combines with appreciation. Gather images, symbols and expressions of gratitude that activate positive emotions elicited from occasions when people expressed gratitude to you. How did it make you feel? Who and what are you grateful for?

If gratitude is one of your top strengths, what do you need to do more often to express gratitude? How can you teach someone to become more aware of and thankful for the good things that have happened recently?

CHALLENGE TO DO NOW

The Gratitude Letter

Write a gratitude letter expressing your appreciation to someone – a family member, friend, or colleague, who inspired or supported you during a difficult time. Tell them you have something special to give them.

Arrange a meeting, read the letter first, then leave it with them. Place a copy in your portfolio and reflect on the thoughts, feeling and emotions aroused. How did the other person respond? Rate your positivity ratio after the meeting.

Books: *The Resilience Project* by Hugh van Cuylenburg or *The Gratitude Effect* by Dr John DeMartini

Movies: *It's a Wonderful Life, August Rush* or *The Color Purple.*

WEEK 3: SERENITY

Every breath we take, every step we make, can be filled with peace, joy, and serenity.

Thich Nhat Hanh

Serenity is a quality or state of being you experience when your mind is clear, uncluttered, and calm. It envelops your being when you are strolling along a quiet beach, meditating in a peaceful place, or listening to the mellow sounds of Gregorian chants. It is when you let out that long even sigh as you sink into a warm bath, relax during a massage, or curl up with a good book. Serenity is a form of detachment, stillness, and inner peace.

Serenity often comes on the heel of other forms of positivity like joy, pride, or awe. It usually emerges when you are in a peaceful place and not rushing about doing things. Paul says it happens when he is abseiling. For Jasim, it occurs when she is playing the piano. Steve feels serene in the afterglow of love making.

Like joy, serenity enters when you feel safe and at one with the world. It requires little effort and emerges in subtle ways: watching the sunset over the pyramids of Giza, sailing the Whitsundays, or listening to a Verdi opera makes you want to sit back and soak it all in. Serenity relaxes your body and tensions melt away.

Being considerate of others, speaking in quite tones and remaining calm under pressure can make us feel serene and content. Whenever I am lazing about listening to ambient music or watching a sunset, I feel calm and serene in every moment. Serenity makes you want to withdraw from the hustle and bustle, be quiet, and soak in the atmosphere.

Serenity is a state of being not doing. One day during a morning walk I stopped at a neighborhood church, entered a small chapel, and knelt to pray with my eyes focused on the flickering red lamp. I breathed deeply, said the Serenity Prayer, and felt a rush of peace and tranquility enter my mind and body. When a young woman sat beside me, I whispered, "This is a special place, isn't it"?

"The best place in the world," she replied with a Mona Lisa smile. When was the last time you savored a serene moment like that? Serenity opens your heart to peace, tranquility, and compassion.

For your 'serenity' portfolio:

➤ Recall occasions when you felt at peace with the world, truly content with where you were, soaking up the atmosphere
➤ Reflect on times when your life felt comfortable and at ease? What were you doing? Who were you with?
➤ Consider how your body feels when you are completely relaxed, with all your physical tensions melted away
➤ Imagine a peaceful place and take it all in, savoring the goodness and luxuriating in peacefulness and tranquility.

Gather resources and create your serenity portfolio. Include spiritual or creative images that awaken your senses: sight, sound, taste, touch, and smell. Decide what you need to do to luxuriate in peacefulness and tranquility, and boost resilience.

CHALLENGE TO DO NOW

Practice Mindfulness for Peace of Mind

To experience peace of mind you could boost your practice with spiritual meditations, by tuning into Nature Sounds, Yoga Nidre or Vipassana (Basic) Meditation on the Insight Timer App.

Repeat the serenity prayer several times a day: *"*May I be granted the serenity to accept the things I cannot change, the courage to change the things I can, and the wisdom to know the difference.*"*

At the end of the week assess your positivity ratio and decide what you need to do more often to reclaim your sense of serenity and flourish the mindful way.

Books: *Book for Serenity* by Thomas Cleary or *Mindfulness* by Mark Williams, and Danny Penman

Movies: E.T. *The Extra Terrestrial*, Seven Years in Tibet or *Eat, Pray, Love*.

Week 4: INTEREST

People with many interests live, not only longest, but happiest.

George Matthew Alle

When something or someone captures your interest, you are utterly fascinated and pulled to explore, to immerse yourself in what you have discovered. It is when you follow a new track in the mountains and want to know where it leads. It is that fascinating movie, new book, or travel experience that captures your attention.

What kinds of things interest you? If you were to wander into a bookshop, under what section would I find you, business or biography, craft or cooking, sport, or self-help? When you pick up the Sunday paper, which section do you read first? What sections do you throw away? How often do you read a new magazine or enroll in a creative course? What is it that draws you in?

Interest awakens passion and fresh ideas. In the movie *Julie and Julia*, Julia Child's story of her start in the cooking profession is intertwined with blogger Julie Powell's challenge to cook all the recipes in Child's first cookbook. Julie's blog also captured the attention of others with similar interests and they joined the challenge.

Interest and curiosity are intertwined. Everyone possesses curiosity to some degree. Yet people differ according to the scope of their curiosity and willingness to act on it. Curiosity builds upon that natural impulse, the same impulse that led you to read this book – the desire to learn more.

Curiosity is a strength related to the receiving of wisdom. It means taking an interest in ongoing experiences for its own sake; finding subjects and topics fascinating; exploring and discovering.

For years, I was interested in politics but never took the time to learn. Until the day I noticed an ad for a course in Australian Politics. The intense pull to learn more drew me in, and I was curious about studying psychology. Five years later, I graduated at the age of 37, majoring in psychology and political science and have never looked back.

When you are interested you feel open and alive. Maybe you have a hobby or special interest you could pursue with gusto? Does psychology, mythology, electronics, antiques, or quantum physics interest you?

For your 'interest' portfolio, consider:

➢ What captures your attention and arouses curiosity? What draws you in by the nose? Which subjects and topics do you find fascinating?
➢ Times when you felt both safe and yet also captivated by something new and unknown. Occasions when you explored or discovered something new?
➢ Your hobbies, special interests and activities that make you feel intensely open and alive. Occasions when you felt an intense pull to explore and learn more, to fully immerse yourself in new discoveries and take in new ideas.

Gather a broad range of resources and compile your interest portfolio. It can be on paper or ephemeral art outside in nature. Consider what you need to do differently to take an interest in the world? Which topics or bodies of knowledge interest you? Is there a special project you have been putting off but could begin today?

CHALLENGE TO DO NOW

Become an Interesting Person

Psychologist Martin Seligman says, "Curious people tend to be attracted to new people, new things, and new experiences, and they are rarely bored." As you become more interested in people, places, and different things, you become a more interesting person.

What could you do today to take an active interest in the world and in your immediate surroundings? Contemplate and add the images to your interest portfolio.

Take time to study the lives of people you find interesting: a scientist, celebrity, or explorer. Decide what you might do to become a more interesting person? If you knew you couldn't fail what new skills or bodies of knowledge would you pursue?

Books: *The Old Curiosity Shop* by Charles Dickens or *Silent Spring* by Rachel Carson.

Movies: *Alice in Wonderland* or *The Best Exotic Marigold Hotel.*

Week 5: HOPE

Fear can hold you prisoner. Hope can set you free.

Movie the Shawshank Redemption

Hope gives you something to look forward to; a wish or secret desire that is accompanied by a confident expectation of its fulfillment. We hope our team wins, that our children will be happy and successful. With hope in your heart, you expect things to work out for the best and you do what needs to be done to achieve it.

Hope shines a light on your potential and strengths to flourish. When you set challenging goals that are in line with your strengths, hope helps you persevere, believe, and achieve. When you're focused and engaged you feel more content and satisfied with your accomplishments. It's a fabulous sensation, better than a runner's high, and more enduring. Hope is linked to optimism and future-mindedness.

Optimistic individuals live in hope. They look on the brighter side of life and maintain a positive attitude even in the face of adversity. Winston Churchill observed that, 'The pessimist sees difficulty in every opportunity. The optimist sees the opportunity in every difficulty.' What kind of a person are you?

Hope can move mountains. It is the stuff dreams are made of. Deep down you believe that a good future is something that can be achieved no matter how difficult the circumstances. In the movie *The Shawshank Redemption* the lead character says, "Fear can hold you prisoner. Hope can set you free."

Hope comes into play when things are not going well. You lose your job and hope the next one will be better. If you have failed an important exam, missed out on a promotion, or sustained a workplace injury, hope helps you move forward.

Believing that a good future is something you can achieve, makes the impossible seem possible. Hope gives you an enduring sense of purpose and the will to excel.

During interviews with elite athletes, prominent leaders, and quiet achievers, I discovered the key strengths they all had in common were hope, optimism and future-mindedness. They knew what they wanted and how to get it. When things went wrong, they did not blame themselves or fall into the pits of remorse. They had their sights set on the future, used their inner resources to overcome adversity, and positive thinking to excel.

What does hope mean, for you?

For your 'hope' portfolio:

➢ Recall a time when you felt hopeful and optimistic, unstoppable, and encouraged by the possibilities of a good outcome. What was your greatest achievement?
➢ Recall situations when you hoped for the best and achieved a goal that made you feel successful and accomplished. What, did you do differently?
➢ When was the last time you yearned for something special to happen? Or imagined it happening? What are your dreams and unfulfilled desires? Write them down.

Gather inspirational resources and create your hope portfolio. Scan popular magazines, tear out pictures that resonate with your desires, and craft a strong collage. Check your strengths profile and note where hope resides. Imagine what you could achieve if you let hope shine its light on you? Consider what you need to do differently to nurture hope in your heart and live with purpose.

CHALLENGE TO DO NOW

Write a Letter to Your Younger Self

Happy endings are commonplace in Hollywood films, and directors like to leave viewers with a sense of hope and positive feelings. Of course, some endings are realistic while others are pure fantasy. If you felt more hopeful, what heights would you aspire to reach?

If you had your life to live over, what would you do differently? Write an imaginary letter to your 16-year-old self and tell that person what they need to do differently to live with hope in their heart and a spring in their step to become the best version of themselves. Check your positivity ratio to see if its elevated. Decide what you need to do differently to seize the day and flourish the mindful way.

Books: *Man's Search for Meaning* by Viktor Frankl, *The Book Thief* by Markus Zusak, or *Letter to my Younger Self* by Jane Graham.

Movies: The Legend of Bagger Vance, The Sound of Music, Cast Away or *Frozen.*

Week 6: PRIDE

Generosity is giving more than you can, and pride is taking less than you need.

Khalil Gibran

Pride has been described as a state or feeling of being proud; a dignified sense of what is due to oneself, one's position or character. It is linked with self-respect, self-esteem, and pleasure, and it feels good.

Your child or grandchildren might be your source of pride and joy. Your art collection might make you feel proud. Knowing you have done your best for a community project or doing good deeds for those less fortunate can boost your self-esteem, and with it comes feelings of pride, altruism, and accomplishment.

Pride is expansive and kindles dreams of bigger things like earning a scholarship, winning an award, lowering your golf handicap, or achieving life-long dreams. When people feel pride, they are more likely to persist with difficult tasks.

Writing a short story and getting it published in a Creative Anthology, gave me an enormous sense of pride, and the positive emotions drive me to excel and achieve.

However, pride is also one of the seven deadly sins and carries with it a mixed reputation. American pro golfer Nancy Lopez takes pride in her accomplishments and distinguishes between genuine and false pride. "A competitor will find a way to win," she says. "Competitors take bad breaks and use them to drive themselves just that much harder. Quitters take bad breaks and use them as reasons to give up. It is all a matter of pride."

In *Pride and Prejudice* novelist Jane Austin likens pride to opinions we have of ourselves. Whereas vanity — or false pride — she says is more about what we would have others think of us. Driving your new Mercedes might give you an after-glow of success or accomplishment, or feelings of false pride if self-esteem is fragile.

Pride carries with it the urge to share the news with others. The day my husband got a hole in one, my son cycled the Tour de France course, my daughter ran a half marathon, and I got a distinction for a short story, I wanted to share the good news with others, celebrate and bask in the power and glory of pride.

Consider what makes you feel proud and purposeful and what you need to do differently to use key strengths such as bravery, judgment, and zest to flourish.

For your 'pride' portfolio reflect on:

➤ Occasions when you felt proud of yourself, confident in your abilities, self-assured and an unstoppable you
➤ A situation when you did something praiseworthy or achieved success through your own efforts. What special attributes did you demonstrate?
➤ Moments of personal glory you wanted to share with others. Small wins
➤ Big dreams and visions of what you might accomplish in the future
➤ Your accomplishments and occasions that filled your heart with pride.

Gather resources and create your pride portfolio. Make a collage of your values and accomplishments and outline a plan for living with passion and purpose. At the end of the week check your positivity ratio to see if it is elevated.

CHALLENGE TO DO NOW

Strengths to Flourish

Having a sense of purpose is the single most important predictor of positivity and longevity that can fill your heart with pride. Review your VIA Signature Strengths Profile at http://www.viame.org. If you have a dream, it's time to begin it now!

Consider three strengths you would like to develop over the next year and set proactive goals to become the best version of yourself. Decide which strengths you most need to muster that will fill your heart with pride. Is it love of learning, bravery, or leadership? Review your goals over time and take pride in your accomplishments.

Books: *The Passion Test* by Janey Bray-Attwood or *The Element* by Ken Robinson

Movies: *Driving Miss Daisy, Forrest Gump, or The Girl with the Dragon Tattoo*

Week 7: AMUSEMENT

You live but once; you might as well be amusing.

Coco Chanel

When I ask people, what amuses them the most, they often smile and reply, "My kids, my family, my dog, my love. Occasionally it is a friend or a secret admirer. Amusement is associated with enjoyment, happiness, laughter, and pleasure.

Amusement brings the irrepressible urge to laugh and share your cheerfulness with others. It often happens unexpectedly when you see the funny side of life and find amusement in small things; a tasteful joke, a comedy or funny story that brings a smile or bouts of laughter. My husband is amusing when he tells a good yarn but even more amusing when he laughs at his own jokes!

It is no joke, laughing may be one of nature's cleverest tricks for keeping us healthy and happy. In 1979, Norman Cousins first captured the attention of the medical community regarding the therapeutic benefits of humor and laughter. After being diagnosed with ankylosing spondylitis – an incurable type of arthritis in the spine that causes a gradual fusing of the vertebrae, he used laughter during his treatment to adapt and change. During long periods in hospital, he watched comedies and laughed his way to recovery, which opened him up to feelings of joy, hope, and love. "Laughter," he said, "was the best medicine."

Amusement is social. Comedian Rowan Atkinson said, "If I can do comedy when I'm very relaxed, and with good friends, then I think I can be amusing." The one thing researchers notice about laughter is that it is something we rarely do alone. When I am with good friends, I can let my hair down, laugh at myself and have a good time. During weekends away we provide our own entertainment just for fun. One time, we shared our bucket lists about growing old together, had a baby guessing photo competition, which was hilarious, and laughed the night away.

Author and playwright *Marilyn Vos Savant once said,* "At first, I only laughed at myself. Then I noticed that life itself is amusing. I've been in a generally good mood ever since." What makes you laugh?

Amusement is infectious and, like chocolate and laugher, it can be addictive. When you have had a good taste of it you want to pass it on to others. What amuses you? When was the last time you had a good belly laugh and let your hair down?

For your 'amusement' portfolio recall:

➢ Occasions when you felt silly and childlike. What amused you? What role did you play?
➢ Times when you laughed uncontrollably? What happened?
➢ Situations when you had the urge to tell a joke, share a funny story or make someone laugh?
➢ People you find amusing and comics who make you laugh. How long did the laughter last?
➢ Times when you let your hair down and acted silly for no reason at all but to have fun and enjoy the moment.

Gather resources: amusing stories, jokes, or cartoons to create your amusement portfolio. Consider what you need to do more frequently to boost your positivity ratio by having fun, letting your hair down, or being amusing. Add images and words that tap into these entertaining and positive emotions.

CHALLENGE TO DO NOW

Lighten Up

Consider what you need to do differently to lighten up and bring more amusement into your life? Watch more funny movies? Join a laughter group? Read light-hearted stories. Learn to draw crazy portrait characters.

Volunteer to become a clown for a day and visit the children's ward of a hospital. Decide what you could do the next time you get together with your friends to have fun and engender infectious laugher. At the end of the week check your positivity ratio.

Books: *Zen and the Art of Motorcycle Maintenance by* Robert M. Pirsig or *Angela's Ashes by* Frank McCourt

Movies: *Amadeus, Life is Beautiful* or *Patch Adams*

Week 8: INSPIRATION

Go confidently in the direction of your dreams! Live the life
you've imagined

Henry David Thoreau

Other than being A-List celebs, what do Colin Farrell, Hugh
Jackman, Angelina Jolie, and Oprah Winfrey all have in
common? They have all changed several people's lives out of
their goodwill and generosity. Inspiration does not simply make
you feel good, it motivates you to do good for others.

Witnessing human nature at its best can inspire, uplift and
change behavior; a friend with terminal cancer who reaches out
to help others is inspiring, a colleague who goes out of his way
to mentor you in a new role can uplift you when the going gets
tough.

Inspiration gains your attention, warms your heart, and draws
you in. It is the opposite of feeling disgusted by human
depravity, which instantly repels you. Inspiration creates the
urge to do your best, so that you can reach your own higher
ground. It is a form of positivity that pulls us out of our own self-
absorption.

One of the best inspirational videos ever was Susan Boyle singing, *I
Dreamed a Dream* during the British *I've Got Talent* show in 2009.
Her stunning and amazing performance was a wake-up call that
stunned the world. Inspirational words, music and images can
inspire and motivate success. They can also tide you through
bad times.

Watching a woman, born with muscular dystrophy swim forty
laps every day without complaint, inspired me to take swimming
lessons when I was forty-two, and persevere until I could swim
forty laps without stopping.

Great thinkers, artists, writers, and entertainers inspire me. Carl Jung, Eckhart Tolle, The Dalai Lama, Leonardo da Vinci, Frida Kahlo, Georgia O'Keeffe, and Nicole Kidman. Who and what inspires you?

Like pride, inspiration has an evil twin. It arises when we see human excellence and respond with negativity, resentment, or envy. When we compare ourselves with a high-flyer or mover and shaker who has done better than us, we can feel discouraged instead of inspired. If this has happened to you be mindful of the evil twin and focus on what you can do to excel for enduring fulfilment.

For your 'inspirational' portfolio reflect on:

➢ Times when you felt truly uplifted or elevated by the wonders of nature
➢ Occasions when you came across true human excellence or virtue
➢ Moments when you saw someone perform far better than you ever imagined
➢ People of excellence who inspire you to achieve. Highlight their strengths.
➢ An image or memory of you at your best? What could you do next to harness your potential and reach your higher ground?

Gather resources and memorabilia and create your inspirational portfolio. Add images of activities, people or places that inspire you or inspire others. Consider what you find inspiring and reflect on ways you can inspire others to let go and grow.

CHALLENGE TO DO NOW

The Artist's Date

Plan an 'Artist's Date' activity and do something different to break the monotony of everyday life. The activity conceived by Julie Cameron in *The Artist's Way* is a block of time, perhaps two hours weekly to nurture your creative consciousness and awaken inspiration. You do not take anyone with you on this occasion, its intention is to open pathways to synchronicities and awaken your kindred spirit.

Suggested activities might include a long country walk, visit to an old book shop, a solitary expedition to the beach for a sunrise or sunset. The choice is yours. Take a notebook and record inspirational ideas to include in your portfolio. At the end of the week check your positivity ratio to see if it is elevated.

Books: *The Vein of Gold* by Julia Cameron or *Inspiration* by Dr Wayne Dyer

Movies: *Bombshell*, *Shindler's List*, *Judy*, or *The Imitation Game*.

Week 9: Awe

*He, who can no longer pause to wonder and stand rapt in awe,
is as good as dead; his eyes are closed.*

Albert Einstein

Awe is closely related to inspiration and wonder. It emerges
when you come across greatness on a grand scale. The seven
wonders of the world, the magnificence of the Grand Canyon,
Notre Dame Cathedral, or the Pyramids of Giza, can stop you in
your tracks, momentarily transfixed and overwhelmed by history
and beauty.

When you come across something that is worthy of your
admiration and respect, you are astonished, amazed, and
impressed. The Tower of London and the awe-inspiring display
of the Crown jewels, the vastness of the great Southern Ocean
and the majesty of the Grand Canyon leave a lasting
impression. Once seen, never forgotten. At other times we're
awed by humans as when we saw Neil Armstrong take his first
steps on the moon and remember his words, "That's one step
for man, and one giant leap for mankind." Can you recall a
moment of grandeur when you were awe struck by something
larger than life?

Awe is related to beauty, wonder, excellence, and elevation.
The beauty of the Sistine Chapel took my breath away; the
excellence of a Verdi opera was unforgettable and watching the
sun set over the Tuscan hills with my daughter, left me feeling
part of something larger than myself. Mentally, I was challenged
to absorb my surroundings, be fully present and soak up the
wonder and glory of it all.

Sometimes awe is mixed with fear. For instance, sitting on the
edge of a cliff during an electrical storm, watching devastating
bushfires take hold in your little corner of the world, witnessing
the collapse of the World Trade Center, leaves us feeling awe
struck and powerless by the sheer force of nature, and people's

evil acts. Fashion designer Vivienne Westwood believed, "The bravery shown by Azza Suleiman who dared to stand up for another woman who was being beaten, and paid a heavy price in doing so, is both awe-inspiring and humbling."

Awe, like gratitude and inspiration is a self-transcendent emotion. It compels us to see ourselves as something much larger than life. In what ways might you use strengths such as appreciation of beauty and excellence or fairness and humility to make a difference in the world?

For your 'awesome' portfolio reflect on occasions when:

➢ You were in awe of nature? Times when you felt intense wonder or amazement, and were deeply aware of your surroundings
➢ You felt overwhelmed by greatness on a grand scale. Occasions when you were mesmerized by beauty excellence and grandeur that surprised you
➢ You were in the wilderness or places like the Grand Canyon, and felt part of something much larger than yourself
➢ Awe-inspiring people or works of art left you lost for words or stunned by the fearlessness of the human spirit.

Gather resources and create your awe portfolio. Include images of what you intend to do more often to boost your positivity ratio by bringing beauty and excellence into your life. From this day forward resolve to open your eyes to the wonders of the world. Use your senses to savor the beauty around you and watch your positivity soar. At the end of the week check your positivity ratio to see if it is elevated.

CHALLENGE TO DO NOW

Activating Awe and Wonder

Set your alarm to get up early and watch the sun rise. Listen to the sounds of nature and awaken your senses. Repeat the process at sunset and observe the kaleidoscope of color on the horizon. Reflect on your thoughts, feelings, and emotions and note how they change as the sun disappears from your sight.

Go to a museum, art gallery or botanic gardens, and look up. Take your camera to record items and installations that capture your attention. Add the photos to your portfolio. Consider what you need to do more often to experience awe and wonder?

Review your strengths profile and decide which strengths you need to master to make a difference in the world? Is it honesty, humility, or teamwork?

Books: *Walking in the World* by Julia Cameron, *The Art of Travel* by Alain de Botton or *I Am Malala* by Christina Lamb and Malala Yousafzai

Movies: *Amelie, Wings of Desire, Midnight in Paris*, *Out of Africa,* or *Samsara.*

Week 10: LOVE

The best and most beautiful things in the world cannot be seen or even touched. They must be felt with the heart.

Helen Keller

Love refers to a variety of different feelings, states, and attitudes, ranging from pleasure — you loved that meal, to interpersonal attraction when you love your partner or fall madly in love with another human or spiritual entity. You might love your children, be in love with your partner, care for your mother and adore your grandmother. Love has been likened to a red rose, a butterfly, and moments of madness. You might be in love with your partner but overcome with rage or jealousy if you feel rejected or unloved. You might learn to love God but become an agnostic.

Whether you agree or disagree that 'love means never having to say you're sorry,' love is an emotion of strong affection and personal attachment and the unselfish and benevolent concern you feel for another. Love is a virtue that represents kindness, compassion, and affection. It is a peak experience, not a single kind of positivity. In *Love 2.0,* Barbara Frederickson describes love as a 'supreme emotion that affects everything, we feel, think, do, and become.'

Love of family is another kind of love that draws me in. It is my top value and one I never take for granted. The joy of birth is an unforgettable peak experience that touches the heart of everyone the world over. I will never forget the raw emotion of love I witnessed after my daughter gave birth to her first child, and her husband cried, "It's a boy… and he's got your nose."

Whilst love might be 'a many splendored thing,' it's also a 'many troubled thing' or so it seems according to Jane Austen. In *Sense and Sensibility*, she shows us dramatically different facets of this crazy little thing called love, from the euphoric to the life-threatening. In that book, love asserts that it, 'Is wonderful and beautiful and all, but there's always a chance it'll creep up behind you and stab you in the back.'

Love is bigger than you and me. You cannot make someone love you, nor can you prevent it, for any amount of money. Love is a force of nature. However much we may want to, we cannot command love, any more than we can command the sun, the moon, the wind, and rain to come and go according to our whims.

Think of times when you felt the surge of love? What were you doing and who were you with? Reflect on the memories and savor the feelings of unforgettable love.

For your 'love' portfolio consider:

➢ The different kinds of love you have experienced in life. How do you view love now? In the past? Or at some time in the future.
➢ What aspects of love elicit expressions of joy, gratitude, or human kindness in your life?
➢ Times when you felt the warmth of love well up between you and another?
➢ How does love playout in your life? What is love for you?
➢ The last time you said, "I love you!" Is there someone you need to show more love towards in the future?

Gather resources and create your love portfolio. Add images that pull at your heart strings and awaken a desire to live and love with passion? Reflect on the positive feeling of love, gratitude and whatever comes up, and make a note of these feelings in your love portfolio.

CHALLENGE TO DO NOW

Seeding Love & Self-Compassion

In the Values in Action Strengths (VIA) classification 'love' is described as: valuing close relationships, those in which sharing, and caring are reciprocated, and being close to people. For the next 21 days practice 'loving kindness' or 'self-compassion' meditation on the Insight Timer app.

At the end of the week check your positivity ratio. Is it elevated? Reflect further on what you need to do to seed more love in your life and flourish the mindful way.

Books: *Pride and Prejudice* by Jane Austin., *Love:2* by Barbara Frederickson, or *Radical Acceptance* by Tara Brach.

Movies: *Casablanca, Doctor Zhivago, Slumdog Millionaire* or *Shakespeare in Love.*

Putting Your Portfolio to Work

The aim of the positivity portfolio is to focus on what you desire and key strengths to flourish. Day by day and week by week, you will learn how to savor memories and experiences that arouse more positive, and less negative emotions. Think of it as building brain power and firing new neurons to flourish mindfully.

As the weeks pass by it is important to monitor your positivity ratio, and watch it rise and fall. Accept there will be challenges and negative emotions. Life is not perfect. Seek support if needed, and practice self-compassion meditation — a self-soothing process to declutter minds, simplify life, and find time to just be.

Finally, after creating your Positivity Portfolio, gaze at it often, savor the positive emotions, and resolve to use your strengths in new ways to flourish. Monitor and watch your positivity ratio soar in an upward spiral, as you broaden and build resilience and draw on your strengths to create a healthier, happier, more vibrant, and flourishing life. The rest is up to you.

Remember life is not a dress rehearsal. You only have one shot at it! So, as the poet Mary Oliver asks, "What are you going to do with your wild and precious life?" Let your portfolio be your inspiration and your guide, to be more authentic, mindful, and fulfilled for the rest of your life.

BONUS GIFT

In case you want a more in depth, step-by-step guide for creating mindfully, I am going to give you a free E book.

The Gift of Mandalas: Creating Luminous Symbols for Personal Growth

E Book Link: http://www.potentialunlimited.com.au

Acknowledgements

Deepest gratitude to:

Tony Miller, Andy Miller, Nicole Nanfra, Mardi Dunbar, Marji Hill, Gabi Plumm, Marcus Amon, Micelle Bolitho, Catherine Chapman, Christine Salins, Judy Paula, Neera Mahajan, Bunny and Kath Earle, my enduring friends, my family, and grandchildren who bring out the best in me. I am forever grateful to these people for their ongoing support and expertise that inspired me to write and publish this book.

About the Author

Barbara Miller is a psychologist and transformational life coach, trained in the field of human development, art therapy and wellbeing. Her strengths include creativity, curiosity, hope and love of learning. She was the founder of the first 'Positive Psychology Interest Group' in Australia and provides Life Coaching Programs for Women online.

With over twenty years of experience as an organisational psychologist and executive coach, she has empowered people from all occupations, to see new possibilities and bounce back stronger from setbacks, by focusing on what's right with them - rather than what's wrong. Thereby being empowered to harness their own potential and achieve meaningful goals for enduring fulfilment.

She lives in Canberra, with her husband Tony and enjoys being part of a large online global community. They have three children, eight grandchildren and spend most of their leisure time travelling in the land down under.

You can find her work, writings, and mandala art on her website at: www.potentialunlimited.com.au

References

Csikszentmihalyi, M. (1990) *Flow: The psychology of optimal experience*. New York: Harper Collins.

Dweck, C. (2006). *Mindset: The new psychology of success.* New York: Random House

Frederickson, Barbara (2009) *Positivity: Top-notch research reveals the 3: 1 ratio that will change your life.* New York: Three Rivers Press.

Niemiec, R and Wedding, D. (2014) *Positive Psychology at the Movies 2nd Ed*. Boston MA: Hogref

Penman, D. (2015) *Mindfulness for Creativity; Adapt, create, and thrive in a frantic world.* London. Piatkus.

Seligman, M. (2011) *Flourish,* Australian: William Heinemann.

Williams, M and Penman, D. (2011) *Mindfulness: An Eight Week Plan for Finding Peace in a Frantic World.* New York: Rodale.

POSITIVE PSYCHOLOGY AND MINDFULNESS

Barbara Fredrickson discusses how positive emotions broaden our awareness of the world, allowing us to become more in tune with the needs of others:
https://www.youtube.com/watch?v=Z7dFDHzV36g&t=167s
(2011)

How mindfulness changes the emotional life of our brains, Ted Talk by Dr. Richard J. Davidson:
https://www.youtube.com/watch?v=7CBfCW67xT8 (2019)

Self-Compassion with Dr Kirsten Neff: https://self-compassion.org

Palouse Mindfulness Meditation, Mindfulness-Based Stressed Reduction: https://palousemindfulness.com

Endnotes

[1] WHO *Depression: Let's talk: Depression tops list of causes of ill health*: https://www.who.int/news

[2] Penman, Danny. (2015:5) *Mindfulness for Creativity*, 2015, Great Britain Piatkus.

[3] Hansen, Sven. (2020) *Resilient Mindset*, Newsletter of The Resilient Institute: https://resiliencei.com.

[4] Goleman, D. & Davidson, R.J. (2017) *Altered Traits*. New York. Every, Random House

[5] Frederickson. B. (2009) *Positivity: Top-Notch Research reveals the 3 : 1 ratio that will change your life*. New   York Three Rivers Press.

[6] Seligman, Martin. (2011) *Flourish*, Australia: William Heinemann.

[7] Mc Niff, S. (1998) *Trust the Process: An Artist's Guide to Letting go*. London: Shambala

www.ingramcontent.com/pod-product-compliance
Lightning Source LLC
Chambersburg PA
CBHW050751290526
45792CB00008B/2137